IT'S MY STATE!

MARYLAND

Steven Otfinoski

Andy Steinitz

Marshall Cavendish
Benchmark
New York

Website: www.marshallcavendish.us

This publication represents the opinions and views of the authors based on their personal experience, knowledge, and research. The information in this book serves as a general guide only. The authors and publisher have used their best efforts in preparing this book and disclaim liability rising directly and indirectly from the use and application of this book.

Other Marshall Cavendish Offices:
Marshall Cavendish International (Asia) Private Limited, 1 New Industrial Road, Singapore 536196 •
Marshall Cavendish International (Thailand) Co Ltd. 253 Asoke, 12th Flr, Sukhumvit 21 Road, Klongtoey Nua, Wattana, Bangkok 10110, Thailand • Marshall Cavendish (Malaysia) Sdn Bhd, Times Subang, Lot 46, Subang Hi-Tech Industrial Park, Batu Tiga, 40000 Shah Alam, Selangor Darul Ehsan, Malaysia

Marshall Cavendish is a trademark of Times Publishing Limited

All websites were available and accurate when this book was sent to press.

Library of Congress Cataloging-in-Publication Data
Otfinoski, Steven.
        Maryland / Steven Otfinoski, Andy Steinitz. — 2nd ed.
               p. cm. — (It's my state!)
        Includes index.
        ISBN 978-1-60870-052-3
        1. Maryland—Juvenile literature. I. Steinitz, Andy. II. Title.
     F181.3.O84 2011
     975.2—dc22   2010003929

Second Edition developed for Marshall Cavendish Benchmark by RJF Publishing LLC (www.RJFpublishing.com)
Series Designer, Second Edition: Tammy West/Westgraphix LLC
Editor, Second Edition: Brian Fitzgerald

All maps, illustrations, and graphics © Marshall Cavendish Corporation. Maps and artwork on pages 6, 24, 25, 75, and back cover by Christopher Santoro. Map and graphics on pages 9 and 43 by Westgraphix LLC. Map on page 76 by Mapping Specialists.

The photographs in this book are used by permission and through the courtesy of:
Front cover: Greg Pease/Getty Images and Driendl Group/Getty Images (inset).
Alamy: Andre Jenny, 10, 54; David Heisler, 11; Michael Ventura, 12; Karen & Ian Stewart, 15; North Wind Picture Archives, 23; Pat & Chuck Blackley, 26, 30; Bill Bachmann, 27; The Print Collector, 31; Irene Abdou, 42; Nick Hanna, 45; WorldFoto, 51, 53; Aayuni, 69. **AP Images:** Todd G. Dudek, 60–61. **Collection of the Maryland State Archives:** Artist: Francis Blackwell Mayer (1827–1899), Title: The Burning of the Peggy Stewart, Date: 1896, Medium: Oil on canvas, Dimensions: 72" x 53", Accession number: MSA SC 1545-1111, 28. **Corbis:** Bettmann, 20; The Mariners' Museum, 22; Richard T. Nowitz, 62. **Getty Images:** John Cornell, 5; Mark Wilson, 13, 40, 49; Paul J. Richards/AFP, 17, 64; Anders Geidemark, 18; Daniel J. Cox, 19 (top); Gabriel Bouys/AFP, 19 (bottom); MPI/Hulton Archives, 29, 46 (left); Thomas D. McAvoy/Time & Life Pictures, 33; Margaret Bourke-White/Time & Life Pictures, 35; Cornell Capa/Time & Life Pictures, 36; Vic Bider, 37; Jon Feingersh, 44; Time & Life Pictures, 46 (right); B. Bennett, 47; Greg Fiume, 50; Matthew Stockman, 52; Richard Nowitz/National Geographic, 57; Mandel Ngan/AFP, 59; Glow Images, 66. **NASA:** Goddard Space Flight Center, 38. **North Wind Picture Archives:** 32. **Shutterstock:** Apaterson, 4; Richard Thornton, 48; David P. Smith, 68; Donald Gargano, 70; Wai Chan, 71 (top); Sebastian Duda, 71 (bottom). **U.S. Air Force:** Tech. Sgt. Ben Bloker, 73. **U.S. Fish and Wildlife Service:** 5, 8, 14, 16, 74.

Printed in Malaysia (T).
135642

MARYLAND

CONTENTS

State Flower: Black-Eyed Susan

This small wildflower is also called the yellow daisy. It is hard to pick the flower without pulling the plant up by the roots because the stems are so tough.

State Crustacean: Blue Crab

The brackish, or slightly salty, water of the Chesapeake Bay is the perfect home for blue crabs. Steamed, sautéed, or cooked in crab cakes or soup, the blue crab is one of Maryland's favorite dishes.

State Bird: Baltimore Oriole

The male oriole's black and orange feathers are the colors of the coat of arms of the Calverts, the English family that founded Maryland. The Baltimore Orioles baseball team is named for this bird.

State Reptile: Diamondback Terrapin

This turtle lives in salty marshes along the Chesapeake Bay. It can be identified by the diamond-shaped rings on its shell. Each shell has a unique pattern. The terrapin is the mascot of the sports teams of the University of Maryland at College Park.

State Tree: White Oak

The white oak was named the state tree of Maryland in 1941. The most famous white oak in Maryland was the Wye Oak. It grew in Talbot County for more than 450 years. The "Quiet Giant" measured nearly 32 feet (10 meters) around. It was downed by a storm in 2002.

State Dog: Chesapeake Bay Retriever

Maryland's state dog is very special. It is one of the few dog breeds native to the United States. It got its name because it is trained to retrieve game birds shot by hunters.

MARYLAND

Baltimore

Nat'l Aquarium

Antietam
Nat'l Battlefield
Site

Fort
McHenry
Nat'l
Monument

Washington
D.C.

Annapolis

U.S. Naval Academy

St.
Mary's
City

Assateague Island

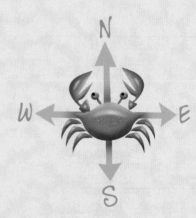

N

W   E

S

Chesapeake
Bay

Atlantic
Ocean

The Old Line State

Maryland is the ninth-smallest state. For such a small state, it has a lot of people. Maryland's population was estimated to be more than 5.6 million in 2007. That made it the nineteenth most populous state. Maryland has a lot of natural wonders to attract all those people—plains, hills, valleys, mountains, and ocean beaches. Forests cover two-fifths of the state. About 160 different kinds of trees thrive there. Maryland has one of the finest bays in the world—the Chesapeake Bay. Proud Marylanders say that their state has it all.

The Chesapeake Bay

No matter where you are in Maryland, you are never very far from water. The Chesapeake Bay nearly cuts the state in half. The regions on either side of the bay are called the Western Shore and the Eastern Shore. The bay is the largest estuary in North America. An estuary is an area where fresh river water and salty ocean water mix. Only 31 miles (50 kilometers) of the

Quick Facts

MARYLAND BORDERS

North	Pennsylvania
South	District of Columbia
	Virginia
East	Delaware
	Atlantic Ocean
West	West Virginia
	Virginia

The 4.3-mile (6.9-km) Chesapeake Bay Bridge connects the Eastern Shore with the Western Shore.

state face the Atlantic Ocean. The Chesapeake Bay, however, provides Maryland with a long and twisting shoreline that runs about 7,000 miles (11,200 km). The bay has many good harbors for boats.

The name *Chesapeake* comes from the Algonquian word *Chesepiooc*. Some people say that was the name of an American Indian village at the mouth of the bay. Others believe the word means "great shellfish bay." Either meaning fits the Chesapeake. For centuries, people have been catching oysters, crabs, and fish in its clear blue waters.

More than four hundred rivers, flowing from six states, feed into the Chesapeake Bay. The largest are the Susquehanna River in the north and the Potomac River, which forms the state's southwestern border. Sixteen of

Maryland's twenty-three counties border the Chesapeake. Annapolis, the state capital, is in Anne Arundel County on the bay's western shore.

There are no natural lakes in Maryland. All existing lakes have been made artificially by damming rivers. The largest of these, Deep Creek Lake, is 12 miles (19 km) long.

Marylanders enjoy all the water that surrounds them. Some like to sail boats in the bay, while others prefer to

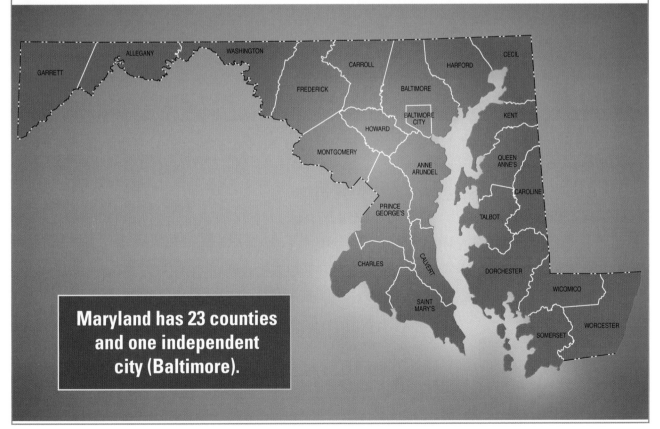

Maryland Counties

Maryland has 23 counties and one independent city (Baltimore).

The Appalachian Region is home to many apple orchards, including this one on Catoctin Mountain.

water-ski. Sport fishing is popular in the Atlantic Ocean, and many people enjoy catching crabs in the bay and rivers.

Plains, Plateaus, and Mountains

Maryland's varied landscape is divided into three land regions. The eastern part—which is split by the Chesapeake Bay—is called the Atlantic Coastal Plain. The area is dotted with marshes and swamps. Much of the fertile land is used for growing crops and raising chickens. The Atlantic Coastal Plain is home to Baltimore, Maryland's largest city. Ocean City, a popular beach town, is also located there. Only about seven thousand residents live in Ocean City year-round, but millions of tourists visit each summer.

Beyond the plains region stretches a wide area called the Piedmont. The plateau's hills and valleys contain most of the state's dairy farms.

A daring kayaker paddles down one of the many rapids of the Great Falls on the Potomac River.

The Appalachian Region is located in the western "panhandle." Two mountain ranges—the Alleghenies and Blue Ridge—are part of the larger Appalachian range. The region's apple orchards thrive in the cooler weather, and its forests provide many jobs. The Appalachians were formed about 230 million years ago. They are the oldest mountains in North America. At Hancock, Maryland, in the Appalachian Region, the state is less than 2 miles (3.2 km) wide from north to south. That is the narrowest width recorded in any state.

The Blue Ridge Mountains extend as far south as northern Georgia and cut across a narrow strip of Maryland. They form one of the loveliest areas of the state. Their name comes from the blue haze that appears to hang over the mountains. The Allegheny Mountains lie in the westernmost part of Maryland. At 3,360 feet

Quick Facts

IT IS ALL DOWNHILL FROM HERE

The Fall Line is a cliff facing the Atlantic Ocean that runs from New Jersey to the Carolinas. In Maryland, it divides the hard rock of the Appalachian Mountains from the soft soil of the Chesapeake. The result is many waterfalls and cascading rapids, such as the Great Falls in Montgomery County.

A young hiker takes a break along the Appalachian Trail in Washington County. The 2,175-mile (3,500-km) trail stretches from Maine to Georgia.

(1,024 m), Backbone Mountain in the Alleghenies is the highest peak in the state.

Climate

Eastern Maryland can be hot and humid in summer. Average temperatures approach 90 degrees Fahrenheit (32 degrees Celsius) in July and August. The area has mild winters, thanks to warm ocean breezes created by the Gulf Stream. The Gulf Stream is a warm ocean current that flows north from the Gulf of Mexico. The mountainous region in the western part of Maryland is considerably cooler and gets the most snowfall in the state. Up to 110 inches (279 centimeters) of snow can fall there every year. The state receives an average of 41 inches (104 cm) of rain a year.

Violent storms and hurricanes are rare in Maryland. An exception was Hurricane Agnes, which struck the Maryland coast in June 1972. In Maryland, the hurricane caused $110 million in damages and took nineteen lives. In September 2003, Hurricane Isabel caused the worst flooding along the Chesapeake coast in seventy years. In Baltimore, water levels rose 8 feet (2.4 m). The storm caused $410 million in damages statewide.

Following Hurricane Isabel, a rescue boat motors down a flooded street in North Beach, on the western shore of the Chesapeake Bay.

Wildlife in Maryland

Maryland once had large wild animals such as cougars, elk, and bison. But people killed or drove away most of them. The only big mammal left in large numbers is the white-tailed deer. Black bears, once a rare site in Maryland, are becoming more common in the western mountains. They have even been spotted on the Eastern Shore. But if you walk through wooded areas, you are more likely to come upon many smaller animals, such as raccoons, muskrats, gray squirrels, and red foxes.

The Chesapeake Bay's marshes are home to thousands of water birds. They include many kinds of ducks, terns, and geese. The great blue heron can be found along the state's many rivers and streams, where it catches fish. With its long, pointed bill and thin, storklike legs, it is the largest American heron.

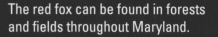

The red fox can be found in forests and fields throughout Maryland.

Maryland hunters stalk game birds, such as quail, mourning doves, and ring-necked pheasants. Hunters often use Maryland's state dog, the Chesapeake Bay retriever, to find the game birds they have shot. No one knows for sure how this dog breed developed in Maryland. One story goes that a British ship was wrecked off the coast in the early 1800s. Two Newfoundland dogs were saved from the ship and bred with local dogs. Over time, they produced a new breed.

Bay retrievers are highly intelligent and very loyal dogs. Sometimes they are trained to sniff out drugs for law enforcement officers and to perform rescue work. These dogs are so friendly that they are brought to hospitals and nursing homes to cheer up patients.

Marylanders have not had as good a relationship with their state bird, the Baltimore oriole. The oriole was given protection under state law in 1882 and was further protected under the state's Nongame and Endangered Species Conservation Act in 1975. Despite these laws, the bird's population has been declining. Much of its habitat has been destroyed by the construction of offices, stores, and factories. Also, many orioles have died from eating insects containing poisonous pesticides.

The Chesapeake Bay is full of many kinds of fish—such as shad, drumfish, and the state fish, rockfish—that are fished commercially. In the ocean, sport fishers hook their lines to catch marlins, which resemble swordfish and can weigh up to 400 pounds (180 kilograms). In the rivers and streams, trout and perch are favorite catches. Marshes are home to the diamondback terrapin, Maryland's state reptile. Before laws were passed to protect them, diamondbacks were nearly hunted into extinction for their delicious meat.

A Chesapeake Bay retriever jumps a hurdle during an agility competition.

DISAPPEARING SHORELINE

Land in the Chesapeake Bay is always changing. The soft soil is moved by the tides. This reshapes the coasts and changes the size of islands. The state loses about 260 acres (105 hectares) of land from erosion every year. St. Clements Island is at the mouth of the Potomac River. Less than a century ago, the island covered 66 acres (27 hectares). Today, it is only 40 acres (16 hectares).

The Wild Horses of Assateague Island

Perhaps Maryland's most interesting animals are the wild horses of Assateague Island. This long, narrow island lies off Maryland's Atlantic coast. Two million visitors come to Assateague Island National Seashore each year to see the horses.

How the horses got there is a mystery. One legend claims that a Spanish ship ran aground on the island many years ago, and the horses on board escaped. But many people now believe the horses are the descendants of workhorses that farmers brought to the island and let graze on the marsh grasses. The grasses are not very nutritious, so the horses of Assateague grow only to the size of ponies.

The wild horses still survive on the marsh grasses today. This has become a problem. The marsh grass holds the sand together to form

Wild horses take a drink at Assateague Island National Seashore.

Horsemen chase a herd of wild Assateague horses across the Assateague Channel to Virginia in 2003. The horses were sold at auction.

dunes. If new dunes are not created, the ocean waters will eat away at the land. One day the island will be covered by water.

Scientists have developed ways to control the wild horse population. State workers shoot darts at the female horses, called mares. The darts contain a vaccine that prevents the mares from having babies. Each year, some of the horses are also rounded up and sold at auctions. These measures keep the number of horses down and help protect the island.

Plants & Animals

Bald Cypress Tree

The bald cypress tree is a relative of the sequoia (suh-KWOY-uh) tree. The Battle Creek Cypress Swamp Nature Center in southern Maryland has one of the northernmost stands of bald cypress in the United States. Some of the trees are more than five hundred years old.

Osprey

About a quarter of America's osprey make the Chesapeake Bay their home during the spring and summer. They feed on the abundant fish in the bay. Their nests can be seen in trees, telephone poles, and other high places.

Great Blue Heron

The great blue heron is the largest kind of heron found in North America. It uses its large pointed bill to catch fish in rivers and streams.

Bobcat

Bobcats look like house cats, but they are twice the size and have dark spots. They can be found in western Maryland. They eat birds, squirrels, mice, and other small animals.

River Otter

The river otter is the only otter found in Maryland. This whiskered mammal likes to make its home on riversides throughout the state. Its eyes have adapted to swimming underwater. River otters have trouble seeing when above water.

Delmarva Fox Squirrel

The Delmarva fox squirrel is one of Maryland's endangered species. This large tree squirrel is shy and quiet. It is not very good at climbing trees and usually runs along the ground when chased by a predator.

From the Beginning

Maryland is the most southern of the Middle Atlantic States. It shares features of both the North and the South. Its people have had divided loyalties going back as far as the American Revolution. Different groups of people in the state were loyal to different causes. Marylanders have usually met history's challenges with courage and determination.

The First Peoples of Maryland

American Indians first came to Maryland around 10,000 BCE. The only hints to their cultures are artifacts such as pottery, arrowheads, and burial sites.

By the 1600s, various Algonquian-speaking tribes were living along the Chesapeake Bay. The Piscataway and Patuxent peoples lived on the Western Shore. The Choptank, Nanticoke, and Assateague lived on the Eastern Shore. The Iroquois-speaking Susquehannock settled in the north at the head of the bay. Some lived in long huts. Others

Quick Facts

THE ALGONQUIAN LANGUAGE
The Algonquian language was spoken by many tribes from the Carolinas to Canada. Some dialects, or versions, of the language are still spoken in North America. However, the dialects that were spoken in Maryland, such as Nanticoke and Piscataway, have long been lost.

Baltimore schoolchildren in the 1940s picket city hall to demand busing to school. Children have played a big role in Maryland's history.

The arrival of European explorers and settlers greatly changed the way of life of Maryland's American Indians.

preferred oval wigwams made from wood and covered with bark or matting. Villages were small and consisted of only several hundred people. The men hunted, fished, and gathered shellfish from the bay. The women grew corn, squash, beans, and tobacco. Many tribes moved inland for the winter. However, European newcomers would soon challenge this traditional way of life.

Explorers and Settlers

Italian explorer Giovanni da Verrazzano may have been the first European to see Maryland. He sailed past the Chesapeake Bay in 1524 while exploring the shoreline of America for the king of France. The first explorer to actually visit the area was Englishman John Smith. In 1608, Smith sailed up the Chesapeake Bay. He described the area that would become Maryland as a "fruitful and delightsome land!"

However, Smith decided to return to the Jamestown colony in Virginia. In 1607, he had helped found the colony, the first permanent English settlement in America. William Claiborne, another member of the

In Their Own Words

[The fish were] lying so thicke with their heads above the waters, as for want of nets we attempted to catch them with a frying pan: but we found it a bad instrument to catch fish with.

—Captain John Smith, after seeing the sea life of the Chesapeake Bay

This painting shows Leonard Calvert planting a cross to mark the settlement of St. Mary's City in 1634.

Virginia colony, also began exploring to the north. He was attracted to the Chesapeake Bay and saw its potential for colonization. Claiborne set up a trading post on Kent Island in the bay in 1631. That was the first permanent European settlement in present-day Maryland.

The next year, King Charles I of England granted the region to George Calvert, the first Lord Baltimore. At the time, many European Protestants and Catholics did not get along. In England, where the rulers were Protestant, laws punished people who practiced Catholicism. England's American colonies had similar laws. Calvert wanted Maryland to be a safe place for Catholics to settle. Calvert died later in 1632, and his son Cecilius Calvert received the land grant. He named the colony Maryland after Charles I's wife, Queen Henrietta Maria, whom the English often called Queen Mary. Cecilius's brother Leonard landed in Maryland with two ships of settlers in March 1634. He founded the settlement of St. Mary's City on the Western Shore. The city became the first capital of the colony.

In 1649, the legislature passed the Act Concerning Religion, which gave all Christians living in Maryland the right to choose how they worshiped. It is one of the first laws granting religious freedom in America.

Quick Facts

SMITH ISLAND
Smith Island is 12 miles (19 km) off the coast of Crisfield in the Chesapeake Bay. It was first settled by the English in the 1600s. The small fishing community has stayed mostly separate from the rest of Maryland. Many islanders still speak with a distinct British accent called a brogue.

MAKING A MODEL LONGHOUSE

When the first European settlers arrived in Maryland, many of the American Indians they encountered lived in longhouses. The longhouse frames were made from two rows of thin poles stuck into the ground. The Indians bent the rows toward each other and tied each pair of poles together. The frame was covered with bark or woven grass mats. Many people lived in each house. You can make a small model of one of these longhouses.

WHAT YOU NEED

Piece of corrugated cardboard, about 9 inches by 9 inches (23 cm by 23 cm)

Plastic wrap

Adhesive tape

Brown clay, about 1 cup

Ten brown or tan pipe cleaners, each 12 inches (30 cm) long

Ruler

Scissors

Brown paper bag

Water

Red or yellow paper

Cover the cardboard square with plastic wrap and tape the plastic wrap down on the back to keep the cardboard dry.

Shape the clay into a ball and place it in the center of the cardboard. Flatten the clay into an oval that is at least 1/4 inch (0.635 cm) thick.

Cut six pipe cleaners into 8-inch (20-cm) lengths and save the extra pieces.

Bend the 8-inch (20-cm) pieces of pipe cleaner into a U-shape, or hoop, with two straight sides and a curved top. Line them up one behind the other, about a finger width apart, with both ends sticking into the clay. Attach one of the remaining 12-inch (30-m) pipe cleaners across the tops of the hoops. Secure it by twisting both ends of the pipe cleaner around the tops of the first and last hoops. Do the same with two other 12-inch (30-cm) pieces, placing them on either side of the first one, about 1 inch (2.5 cm) away.

Cut a piece of brown paper bag to fit over the top of the longhouse, from the ground on one side to the ground on the other. Cut two more pieces of the bag to cover the ends. Make sure the cut pieces are the same size and shape as the ends of the longhouse. Cut a doorway in one of the end pieces.

To make the paper look more like bark or grass, crumple each piece, wet it, and then flatten it out. Lay the biggest piece over the longhouse top so it dries in the shape you want. When the paper is dry, attach a piece of tape to the inside of the long piece, so that about 1 inch (2.5 cm) of tape hangs off the end. Hold one of the end pieces of paper in place. Attach the end piece to the tape that is hanging off the end of the long piece. This way the tape will not show. Repeat these steps for the other end piece. You may use several pieces of tape to make sure the paper stays in place, but you do not need to tape the paper to the frame.

Make a "fire" inside the longhouse with tiny bits of pipe cleaner as logs and colored paper as flames.

Visitors can learn about colonial Maryland at the Thomas Stone National Historic Site, a restored plantation from the 1770s.

A Growing Colony

The Calvert family ruled the Maryland colony despite several disputes, including a feud with Claiborne over Kent Island. In 1689, colonists seized the government and demanded that the king take over the colony. The first royal governor arrived in 1692. Two years later, the capital was moved from St. Mary's City to Anne Arundel Town. Later, its name would be changed to Annapolis.

Maryland farmers started tobacco plantations along the rivers that empty into the Chesapeake Bay. They needed many workers for these big farms. Africans were first brought to Maryland by ship in the 1600s. Then, in 1664, slavery—the enslavement of blacks for life—became legal in the colony. But before the 1700s, both black and white indentured servants were more common than slaves. Indentured servants were people whose passage to America was paid in exchange for work for a master, usually for up to seven years. After that period, the servant was freed. Mathias de Sousa was a black indentured servant who arrived with the first colonists in 1634. He soon gained his freedom and in 1642, he became the first black man to serve in the state's general assembly.

By the 1700s, African slaves had replaced most white indentured servants on the large tobacco plantations. Most of the slaves led miserable lives. They were forced to work long hours six days a week. They were housed in shabby cabins and given awful food.

The colony continued to grow. During the 1700s, European settlers forced many American Indians to move west, out of Maryland. Some American Indians were killed when they refused to give up their land. Others died of diseases brought by the settlers from Europe. Today, only about five thousand American Indians live in the state.

The city of Baltimore, founded in 1729, became a center where farmers could sell their goods. In the 1760s, Maryland quarreled with Pennsylvania over its border. That dispute included Pennsylvania's three lower counties, which are now the state of Delaware. The British government sent Charles Mason and a surveyor, Jeremiah Dixon, to mark the boundary line between the two colonies. A surveyor is a person who measures the size and position of a piece of land. Completed in 1767, their survey was used less than a decade later to separate the states of Maryland, Delaware, and Pennsylvania. In the 1800s, the Mason-Dixon Line became a symbolic border between Northern "free" and Southern slave states.

Stone markers like this one were built in the 1760s to note the boundaries established by the Mason-Dixon Line.

The American Revolution

A larger conflict was growing between Great Britain and its American colonies. While tobacco farmers and some other Marylanders were on good terms with

This painting shows the burning of the *Peggy Stewart* by Maryland colonists in October 1774.

the British, many colonists wanted independence. In 1774, Maryland patriots in Annapolis copied the Boston Tea Party of 1773. They protested the British tax on tea by burning a British ship, the *Peggy Stewart*, and its cargo of tea.

War broke out in April 1775. Not much fighting took place in Maryland during the American Revolution. Maryland soldiers, however, fought bravely in many battles.

The colonists won their independence in 1783. The Thirteen Colonies—now states—struggled to find a new form of government. In September 1786, Annapolis hosted a states' convention. Delegates discussed the issues of trade and business. They agreed to meet again in Philadelphia in 1787.

At the Philadelphia convention, delegates wrote the U.S. Constitution. It was a bold plan for a national government. On April 28, 1788, Maryland became the seventh state to ratify, or approve, the new Constitution.

"The Second American Revolution"

In 1812, the United States once again went to war with Great Britain. People sometimes call the War of 1812 the second American Revolution. This time a good deal of fighting took place in Maryland. In 1813, the British entered the Chesapeake Bay, attacking ships and raiding towns. In September 1814, one month after British forces burned much of Washington, D.C., they attacked

Baltimore. American lawyer Francis Scott Key was aboard a truce boat, awaiting the release of an American doctor imprisoned by the British. From the boat, he watched the British bombard Fort McHenry, which guards the entrance to Baltimore harbor. All day and into the night on September 13, Key watched British ships fire rockets and exploding bombs at the fort.

To Key's joy, the next morning the American flag still flew over the fort "by the dawn's early light." The British retreated. Key began to write a poem about the event, which he finished that night. Less than a week later, his poem, "Defense of Fort McHenry," was published in a Baltimore newspaper. It was later set to the tune of an English song and became "The Star-Spangled Banner." In 1931, eighty-eight years after Key's death, his patriotic song officially became the U.S. national anthem.

The United States and Great Britain signed a peace treaty ending the War of 1812 in December 1814. (Because news traveled slowly at that time, a major American victory in the war, at the Battle of New Orleans, actually took place in January 1815.)

This painting from the 1800s shows a woman who symbolizes America holding the American flag, or star-spangled banner.

The LaVale Toll Gate House in LaVale, Maryland, was built along the National Road in the 1830s.

The Civil War

The 1800s saw Maryland make great strides in industry and development. The first national highway, called the National Road, was finished in 1818. It joined Cumberland, Maryland, with Wheeling, Virginia (now in West Virginia). Peter Cooper built one of the first American steam locomotives, *Tom Thumb*. The locomotive made its first run on the new Baltimore & Ohio Railroad in 1830. In 1844, Samuel Morse sent the first message over a telegraph line from Washington, D.C., to Baltimore.

All these achievements helped bring Americans closer together, but the issue of slavery moved them farther apart. By the mid–1800s, most people in the North opposed slavery. In the South, most people supported it. Harriet Tubman, a runaway slave from Maryland, helped many other slaves escape from the South. She was the most famous "conductor" on the Underground Railroad, a network of secret routes and people who helped slaves travel from one "station," or safe hiding place, to another on their way to freedom in the North.

By early 1861, a number of Southern states had seceded, or broken away, from the United States, or Union. They formed the Confederate States of America. The people of Maryland were torn. Many wanted Maryland to remain in the Union, and it did. Yet some still relied on slave labor, and many sided with the Confederacy. On April 19 in Baltimore, a mob of pro-Confederates attacked troops from Massachusetts who were traveling to Washington, D.C. Four soldiers and twelve other people died in the riot. They were the first people killed in the Civil War. (The first shots of the war had been fired a week earlier when

This illustration shows slaves escaping from Maryland to Delaware by way of the Underground Railroad.

In Their Own Words

I was the conductor of the Underground Railroad for eight years, and I can say what most conductors can't say—I never ran my train off the track, and I never lost a passenger.

—Harriet Tubman

Confederate forces attacked Fort Sumter in South Carolina).

More than 70,000 Maryland soldiers fought in the war. About 50,000 of them fought for the Union. Several important battles were fought in the state. The biggest was the Battle of Antietam on September 17, 1862.

Confederate general Robert E. Lee had invaded Maryland with 37,400 troops two weeks earlier. Under General George McClellan, 56,000 Union soldiers met them at Antietam Creek near Sharpsburg. The fighting began in the early morning and continued throughout the day. When the battle ended—with a Union

CIVIL RIGHTS PIONEER

Frederick Douglass was born a slave on a plantation in Talbot County, Maryland. He was separated from his mother before he was ten. As a servant in Baltimore, he was taught the alphabet, and then taught himself to read and write. Douglass escaped to freedom in Massachusetts, where he spoke out against slavery. His autobiography shared the plight of slaves with thousands of readers in the United States and Europe. During the Civil War, Douglass advised President Abraham Lincoln about issues faced by black soldiers.

victory—more than 23,000 soldiers on both sides were wounded or dead. It was the bloodiest one-day battle of the Civil War.

After Antietam, Lee retreated to Virginia. The Union victory gave President Abraham Lincoln the opportunity to issue an early version of his Emancipation Proclamation. In the final proclamation, effective January 1, 1863, Lincoln declared that all slaves in Confederate-controlled territory "shall be then, thenceforward, and forever free."

In 1864, Maryland adopted a new state constitution that abolished slavery. It also denied Confederate supporters the right to

Union and Confederate troops face off at the Battle of Antietam.

vote. The war ended in Union victory the following year. In December 1865, the Thirteenth Amendment to the U.S. Constitution officially ended slavery throughout the United States.

Growth and Reform

In the years following the Civil War, Maryland became a leader in science and education. Johns Hopkins University was founded in Baltimore in 1876. The world-famous Johns Hopkins Hospital opened thirteen years later. Today, the hospital and school remain important research centers. Johns Hopkins doctors have discovered new treatments for tuberculosis and other diseases. In 1886, Baltimore established one of the first free public library systems in the country.

Since its opening in 1889, Johns Hopkins Hospital in Baltimore has been one of the leading medical centers in the United States.

PIONEERS OF FLIGHT

College Park is the oldest airport in the world. It opened in 1909 as an Army training facility. There, Wilbur Wright trained pilots to fly the U.S. military's first airplane. In 1903, Wright and his brother Orville had made the world's first powered flights in an airplane, in Kitty Hawk, North Carolina.

Maryland at War

The United States entered World War I in 1917. More than 62,000 Marylanders served in the armed forces. The U.S. Army established Aberdeen Proving Ground near the Chesapeake Bay in 1917 to test new weapons. Today, it is the oldest active proving ground. In Anne Arundel County, the War Department established a base that became known as Fort Meade. During the war, more than 400,000 soldiers passed through Fort Meade, which remains a major Army base today.

Prohibition

In 1919, the Eighteenth Amendment to the U.S. Constitution banned the manufacture, sale, and transportation of alcoholic beverages throughout the country. The period when alcohol was illegal is called Prohibition. The Maryland state government did not want the federal government telling Marylanders what to do. (Prohibition was not very popular with many Americans and was repealed by another constitutional amendment in 1933.) During Prohibition, Marylanders were encouraged to defy the law by their own governor, Albert C. Ritchie. Legend has it that this fierce independence earned Maryland the nickname the Free State.

Depression and More War

During the 1930s, the Great Depression caused great hardship for Marylanders and people across the country. Thousands of banks failed, businesses closed, and millions of people were out of work. The U.S. government created many new

Women work as welders in a Maryland steel mill during World War II.

programs to help the nation recover. In Maryland, the government built a new town, called Greenbelt, not far from Washington, D.C. Building the town created new jobs and gave people affordable places to live.

On December 7, 1941, the Japanese bombed the U.S. naval base in Pearl Harbor, Hawaii. The USS *Maryland*, named after the state, was one of the battleships damaged in the attack. The next day, the United States entered World War II. During the war, some 55,000 Marylanders served in the armed forces. Many more worked in shipbuilding, aircraft manufacturing, and other wartime industries. Women took over the jobs of many men who were called to fight overseas. After the war ended in 1945, the state had more jobs than people to fill them. Maryland's cities and towns grew bigger than ever. From 1940 to 1950, the state's population grew by more than 500,000.

Struggle for Freedom

Despite the state's growing prosperity, many African Americans felt left behind. Like many other states, Maryland had laws that forced blacks and whites to use

Thurgood Marshall was one of the most important figures in the fight for civil rights.

separate public facilities, such as train cars, restaurants, and schools. In this system of separation, or segregation, the quality of services offered to blacks was not as good as what was offered to whites. Maryland's African Americans had long been fighting to gain the same treatment as whites. The National Association for the Advancement of Colored People (NAACP) is an organization that fights for civil rights. The NAACP's second-oldest chapter had been founded in Baltimore in 1913. Baltimore is now the organization's home.

NAACP attorney Thurgood Marshall, from Baltimore, was a leader in the fight for civil rights. In 1954, he won a U.S. Supreme Court decision against segregation in public schools. In 1967, President Lyndon Johnson appointed Marshall to the U.S. Supreme Court. He was the first African American to receive that honor. Marshall served on the Court for twenty-four years before retiring in 1991 at age eighty-three.

Though African Americans had made gains in racial equality, their struggle was far from over. Civil rights leader Martin Luther King Jr. was assassinated in Memphis, Tennessee, in 1968. His murder led to riots in Baltimore and other U.S. cities. The riots had a lasting negative effect on Baltimore, which was already struggling. The city's population had peaked in the years after World War II. In 1950, Baltimore was the sixth-largest city in the United States. But as large numbers of white people moved to neighboring areas, or suburbs, the population began to fall.

As suburbs prospered, Balitmore began to suffer. Many African Americans either could not afford to move to suburbs or were not allowed to because of discrimination. The manufacturing jobs that had been so vital to the city's economy disappeared.

The economy of the whole state suffered in the 1970s. Many businesses closed or moved to other states, leaving thousands of Marylanders out of work.

Rebuilding Baltimore

In the 1970s, the government took steps to attract businesses and tourism to Baltimore. In the mid–1970s, the city celebrated the opening of the Baltimore Convention Center and the Baltimore World Trade Center—the tallest building with five even sides (pentagon) in the world. In 1980, a new business area called Harborplace opened in what had become a run-down area of the old harbor (or Inner Harbor) in Baltimore. Tourists flocked to its shops and restaurants. The National Aquarium opened in the Inner Harbor district the following year. In the 1990s, the city built new stadiums for its

Baltimore's Inner Harbor area is one of the biggest tourist attractions in the state.

The visitor center at the Goddard Space Flight Center has popular exhibits about the study and exploration of space.

baseball team, the Orioles, and its new professional football team, the Ravens. But even as tourism increased, the city's population continued to fall. In 2008, Baltimore ranked twentieth in the nation.

Maryland Today

Today, Maryland is home to many high-tech industries. Light technology such as computers, lab work, and scientific research has replaced heavy industry in its cities. The federal government has many scientific agencies that are headquartered in Maryland. The National Institutes of Health in Bethesda performs medical research. Scientists and engineers at the Goddard Space Flight Center in Greenbelt develop new instruments and technology to study Earth and outer space. The Old Line State has moved into the twenty-first century with renewed confidence.

Important Dates

★ **1524** Italian explorer Giovanni da Verrazzano sails past Chesapeake Bay.

★ **1608** Englishman John Smith explores Chesapeake Bay and maps it.

★ **1631** William Claiborne founds the first permanent European settlement in what is now Maryland, on Kent Island.

★ **1649** The Act Concerning Religion, one of the first laws granting religious liberty in America, is passed.

★ **1729** Baltimore is founded.

★ **1774** To protest British taxation, patriots in Annapolis burn a British ship carrying tea.

★ **1788** Maryland ratifies the U.S. Constitution on April 28 and becomes the seventh state.

★ **1814** The British attack Maryland during the War of 1812. American soldiers defend Baltimore in September, inspiring Francis Scott Key to write "The Star-Spangled Banner."

★ **1830** The Baltimore & Ohio Railroad begins service as the first railway in the United States.

★ **1862** The Battle of Antietam is fought in Sharpsburg on September 17.

★ **1876** Johns Hopkins University is founded in Baltimore.

★ **1952** The Chesapeake Bay Bridge opens.

★ **1967** Marylander Thurgood Marshall is appointed to the U.S. Supreme Court.

★ **1968** Maryland governor Spiro T. Agnew is elected vice president of the United States.

★ **1980** Harborplace opens in Baltimore's Inner Harbor.

★ **2000** Maryland, Virginia, Pennsylvania, and the District of Columbia sign the Chesapeake Bay Agreement, setting standards for the bay's restoration.

★ **2001** The Baltimore Ravens win their first Super Bowl.

★ **2008** Maryland native Michael Phelps wins a record eight gold medals at the Olympics in Beijing, China.

The People

Maryland's residents come from a wide range of cultures. Many share heritages brought by their European ancestors. These include the Irish, Germans, English, Italians, and Polish. People with roots in India, Mexico, China, and other Asian and Latin American nations celebrate their own rich cultures. Some have lived in Maryland all their lives, while others are new to the state. No matter how long people have lived in the state, the blending of their cultures, beliefs, and abilities has helped make Maryland a unique place to live and work.

Many businesses that specialize in ethnic foods and other goods bring an international flavor to Maryland. Langley Park near Washington, D.C., is one of the many cities that have growing Hispanic communities. In places like these, American traditions are mixed with cultures from the Caribbean and from Mexico, Central America, and South America. Across the state, festivals and other cultural celebrations are also held throughout the year. Baltimore alone hosts Polish Festival, LatinoFest, Fest Africa, India Festival, and more.

American Indians

Before the Europeans arrived, there were more than twenty American Indian groups on the land that is now Maryland. Many tribes were forced to move as Europeans began to settle in the area. Today, less than one-tenth of one percent of Maryland's population is American Indian.

A young Marylander cools off under a waterfall at Chesapeake Beach Water Park.

Before the American colonies were established, the Accohannock Tribe lived on the eastern shores of Maryland and Virginia. The tribe is currently trying to obtain federal recognition. Such recognition would enable the tribe to claim a legal relationship to the U.S. government and receive federal aid.

Every year, the tribe holds the Native American Heritage Festival and Powwow. At this event, the Accohannocks celebrate their traditions and culture. Members of the tribe also attend powwows in other states and present their culture to schools and other organizations.

African Americans

African Americans are Maryland's largest minority. They make up about 30 percent of the population. In Baltimore, nearly two-thirds of the residents are black. A number of African Americans have moved from Washington, D.C., to nearby

An American Indian dancer performs at the Healing Horse Spirit Powwow in Mount Airy, Maryland, in 2008.

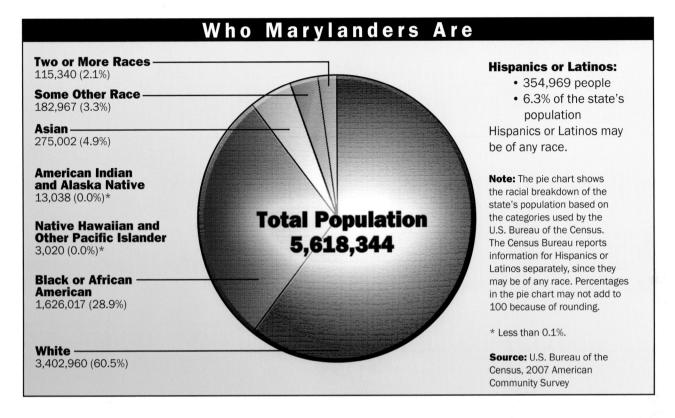

Who Marylanders Are

Two or More Races
115,340 (2.1%)

Some Other Race
182,967 (3.3%)

Asian
275,002 (4.9%)

American Indian and Alaska Native
13,038 (0.0%)*

Native Hawaiian and Other Pacific Islander
3,020 (0.0%)*

Black or African American
1,626,017 (28.9%)

White
3,402,960 (60.5%)

Total Population 5,618,344

Hispanics or Latinos:
- 354,969 people
- 6.3% of the state's population

Hispanics or Latinos may be of any race.

Note: The pie chart shows the racial breakdown of the state's population based on the categories used by the U.S. Bureau of the Census. The Census Bureau reports information for Hispanics or Latinos separately, since they may be of any race. Percentages in the pie chart may not add to 100 because of rounding.

* Less than 0.1%.

Source: U.S. Bureau of the Census, 2007 American Community Survey

Prince George's County in southeastern Maryland. Once mostly white, Prince George's County is now more than 65 percent black. Wayne K. Curry was the first African American to hold the county's executive position. He served from 1994 to 2002.

In 2003, Michael Steele became Maryland's lieutenant governor. That is the second-highest office in the state government. Steele was the first African American to be elected to a statewide office in Maryland. He is a member of the Republican Party—one of the two main political parties in the United States. (The other is the Democratic Party.) In 2009, Steele became the first African American to chair the Republican National Committee, which sets the party's goals and values.

City of Neighborhoods, Museums, and Music

About nine of every ten Marylanders live in or near a city. The rest live in rural areas. Annapolis, the state capital, is small. It has only about 36,000 people.

African Americans, young and old, make up a large percentage of Maryland's population.

Baltimore is the state's largest city, with a population of more than 630,000.

Baltimore is known as the city of neighborhoods. Many of those neighborhoods were formed in the 1800s by European immigrants who wanted to live near people from their homelands. They wanted to be able to speak their native languages and help each other find jobs and places to live. Today, there are more than 225 neighborhoods in the city.

Many Irish once lived in southwestern Baltimore. They helped build the Baltimore & Ohio Railroad. The houses they once lived in were supposed to be torn down. However, local residents worked to restore them. The railroad's old engine roundhouse nearby has been turned into a museum. A roundhouse is a circular building that is used for storing and repairing locomotives.

Another museum in Baltimore is dedicated to African Americans. The National Great Blacks in Wax Museum has more than a hundred life-size wax figures of famous Maryland African Americans. One of the figures is of Matthew Henson. In 1909, he became the first explorer to reach the North Pole, as part of an expedition led by Robert Peary. The museum also has a large model of a slave ship.

Visitors explore the popular Australia exhibit at the National Aquarium in Balitmore.

Downtown Baltimore has many things to see, such as Harborplace and Camden Yards, the home of the Orioles baseball team. The National Aquarium is seven stories high and has an Atlantic coral reef with 335,000 gallons (1.3 million liters) of water and hundreds of tropical reef fish. Visitors can also walk through a South American rain forest encased in glass or explore an Australian Outback river gorge.

Music lovers may enjoy the Baltimore Symphony Orchestra, which plays classical music. Fans of jazz can see live performances at the Eubie Blake National Jazz Institute and Cultural Center. Eubie Blake was a famous ragtime and jazz composer who was popular in the early twentieth century.

Famous Marylanders

Benjamin Banneker: Scientist and Writer

Born in 1731, Benjamin Banneker was probably the most famous African American of the 1700s. He was a farmer, a mathematician, an astronomer, an almanac writer, and a surveyor. Thomas Jefferson was impressed by Banneker's abilities and asked him to help survey the new capital in Washington, D.C. "The powers of the mind," wrote someone who knew Banneker, "are disconnected with the color of the skin."

Edgar Allan Poe: Writer

Edgar Allan Poe was born in Boston in 1809, but he lived with his wife in Maryland for several years. He wrote poetry and horror stories such as "The Tell-Tale Heart" and "The Black Cat." Poe is known as the writer of the first modern detective stories. He died in Baltimore in 1849 and was buried in the city's Westminster Hall and Burying Grounds. Baltimore's professional football team, the Ravens, is named after his most famous poem, "The Raven."

Harriet Tubman: Abolitionist

Harriet Tubman was born into slavery in Maryland in the early 1800s. After escaping to the North, she was part of the Underground Railroad and helped many other runaways from Maryland and other slave states. After the Civil War, she settled in New York, where she fought for women's rights and for better living conditions for the elderly and the poor.

Babe Ruth: Baseball Player

Born in Baltimore in 1895, George Herman "Babe" Ruth was one of the greatest baseball players who ever lived. The Sultan of Swat, as he was called, was the first great home-run hitter. Playing for the New York Yankees, he hit 60 home runs in 1927. This record was not broken until 1961 by Roger Maris. Ruth hit a total of 714 home runs in his career. His skill and colorful personality helped attract countless new fans to baseball.

Billie Holiday: Singer

Billie Holiday was one of America's great jazz singers. Born in Philadelphia in 1915, she was raised in Baltimore and later moved to New York. There, she began to sing in local clubs. At age eighteen, Holiday made her first record. Musicians respected her ability to express the pain and loneliness in her life through her singing. They called her Lady Day. In her later years, Holiday was addicted to drugs and alcohol, but she kept singing almost until her death at age forty-four.

Michael Phelps: Swimmer

Born in Baltimore in 1985, Michael Phelps learned to swim at the North Baltimore Aquatic Club. He swam in his first Olympics in 2000, when he was just fifteen. He won eight medals, including six golds, at the 2004 Olympics in Athens, Greece. At the 2008 Olympics in Beijing, China, Phelps won gold medals in all eight events in which he competed. That is a record for the most golds won by an individual in a single Olympics.

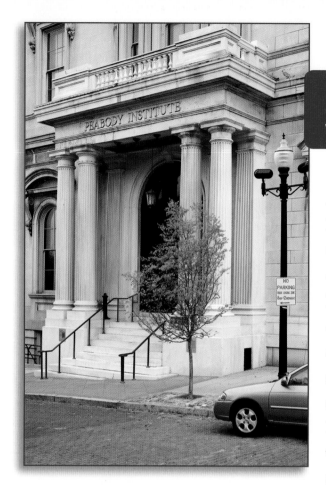

Founded in 1857, the Peabody Institute is part of Johns Hopkins University. The institute is a well-known music school.

A Leader in Education

Education is important in Maryland. One of the first U.S. public high schools opened in Baltimore in 1839. Western High School, which opened in 1844, is the oldest all-girls public high school in the country. There are more than 1,400 public schools and more than 1,200 private schools throughout the state. Since 2003, Maryland has funded charter schools as well. Charter schools are public schools (tax-supported) run by independent groups rather than local school boards. They have specific educational goals. In 2008, a higher percentage of Maryland high school students passed their Advanced Placement (AP) exams than in any other state. Students who pass AP exams can earn credit toward a college degree.

Quick Facts

MAKING A BETTER FUTURE

Founded in 1876, Johns Hopkins University was the first modern research university in the nation. Among other achievements, faculty members developed the process of chlorinating tap water to kill many disease-carrying bacteria. They also discovered the medication heparin, which keeps blood from clotting and is used to treat patients who suffer from blood clots. Other researchers developed the sugar substitute saccharine and the moisture-absorbing gel that preserves bags of snacks.

First-year students at the U.S. Naval Academy in Annapolis take part in a demanding training exercise.

More than one in three adult Marylanders is a college graduate. That is one of the highest percentages in the nation. Today, college-bound students can choose from more than a dozen universities in Maryland. Since 1999, students have been able to take college courses on the Internet.

George Washington helped found the first college in the state in 1782. It is called Washington College in his honor. Mount St. Mary's in Emmitsburg is the country's second-oldest Catholic college. The University of Maryland in College Park is the largest college in the state, with more than 30,000 students. It was founded on a former plantation in 1859. The University of Maryland, Baltimore County, is one of the most diverse colleges in the country. A large percentage of its students are either Asian American or African American. Annapolis is the home of the U.S. Naval Academy. Cadets spend their summers training on ships at sea. When they graduate, cadets become officers in the U.S. Navy or the Marine Corps.

Young Baltimore Orioles fans check out the field at Camden Yards before a game in April 2009.

Sports and Recreation

Marylanders like to work and study, but they also like to play. The state is home to the Baltimore Orioles baseball team and the Baltimore Ravens football team. The Redskins football team may be from Washington, D.C., but the team plays its home games in Landover, Maryland. A half-dozen minor league baseball teams are also based in the state, from the Hagerstown Suns to the Delmarva Shorebirds in Salisbury.

Horse racing has been a tradition at Pimlico Race Course in Baltimore since 1870. The first Preakness Stakes was held three years later. Tens of thousands of fans still crowd the stands and the track's grassy infield to watch the Preakness. It is the second race of horse racing's Triple Crown series.

Annapolis's beautiful harbor is one of the top centers for sailing on the East Coast. Visitors can sail aboard the schooner *Woodwind*, a replica, or copy, of a luxury yacht from the early 1900s. During their tour of the harbor, amateur sailors can help the crew raise the sails and even take turns steering the ship.

One of the state's most popular sports—lacrosse—is the oldest team sport in North America. It was invented by American Indians. Each player uses a stick with a net attached at one end to throw a ball into the opposite team's goal. Johns Hopkins University, the University of Maryland, Baltimore County, and the University of Maryland, College Park, have some of the best men's college lacrosse teams. The powerhouse University of Maryland Lady Terrapins have won more lacrosse national championships than any other team.

Maryland's state sport is jousting. This sport was developed in the Middle Ages when knights on horseback tried to knock each other to the ground with long metal-tipped wooden spears called lances. Marylanders have enjoyed jousting since colonial times. They play a less violent form of jousting. Riders attempt to "spear" hanging rings with a lance. Each rider must do this while galloping on horseback. The one who lifts the most rings is the champion.

A lacrosse player from the University of Maryland Terrapins tries to push past a defender.

Calendar of Events

★ Annual Maple Syrup Demonstration

Every year this March festival is held in Cunningham Falls State Park. Visitors can enjoy tree-tapping and sap-boiling demonstrations, a pancake breakfast with fresh syrup, storytelling, and other activities.

★ The Maryland International Kite Exposition

This weekend event is held in April in Ocean City. It features kites of all kinds, colors, and sizes. Among the many contests are a stunt kite championship and a kite makers' competition.

★ The Preakness Celebration

The Preakness Stakes is held every May at Pimlico Race Course in Baltimore. It is one of the most famous horse races in the country. The Preakness Celebration includes parades, concerts, and fireworks.

★ HonFest

The Baltimore neighborhood of Hampden shows its city pride in June. *Hon* is short for "Honey," a friendly term used by locals. The lady with the biggest hair, best personality, and most "Bawlmer" accent is crowned Miss Hon.

★ Fiddle and Banjo Contest

Held in July in Friendsville, this friendly competition features musicians playing country and bluegrass music. It also showcases traditional styles of dancing called clog and buck-and-wing.

★ The Maryland State Fair

For eleven days in August, Timonium hosts the state fair, which includes livestock shows, rides, arts and crafts, music, horse racing, and contests. At the birthing center, visitors can see local farmers' cows and pigs give birth to their young.

★ Skipjack Race and Festival

During Labor Day weekend, many people gather on Deal Island for this event. Activities include arts and crafts, contests, and the annual skipjack races—which honor the official state boat. A skipjack is a small boat with one mast and a V-shaped bottom.

★ The National Hard Crab Derby

This September celebration in Crisfield includes crab-picking and crab-cooking contests, a plastic boat regatta, and, of course, the crab derby. In the derby, crabs with numbered shells race each other across the ground.

★ The State Jousting Championship

Held at different locations across the state every October, this event has men, women, and children competing in ring tournaments.

How the Government Works

L ike all states, Maryland has different levels of government: town or city, county, and state. At each level, the government makes and enforces laws for its residents.

Local Government

Maryland is divided into twenty-three counties. In each county, one city or town is the county seat. Elected officials meet there to make county laws. City councils or county commissioners enforce the laws. The county government runs some towns and cities that are unincorporated. An unincorporated community does not have its own government. It does not have its own police department and other services and must rely on the county to provide them. Towns and cities that are incorporated are run by their own governments.

Baltimore, Maryland's largest city, is not part of a county. It is an independent municipality run by a mayor and a city council. That is unusual, except in Virginia. The rest of the United States has only three independent cities: Baltimore; St. Louis, Missouri; and Carson City, Nevada.

State Government

The state government has a similar structure to that of the federal (national) government. Both are divided into an executive branch, a legislative branch,

This photo shows the interior of the house of delegates chamber in the State House in Annapolis.

Branches of Government

EXECUTIVE ★ ★ ★ ★ ★ ★ ★ ★

The governor is the head of the executive branch. He or she carries out laws and appoints people to high office. The governor is elected to a four-year term. He or she can serve only two terms in a row.

LEGISLATIVE ★ ★ ★ ★ ★ ★ ★ ★

This branch makes the state's laws. Maryland's legislature is called the General Assembly. It is divided into two parts. The senate has forty-seven members, and the house of delegates has 141 members. All General Assembly members are elected to four-year terms. There is no limit on the number of terms they can serve.

JUDICIAL ★ ★ ★ ★ ★ ★ ★ ★

The judicial branch interprets and enforces the laws. When a person is accused of breaking a law, he or she goes on trial in one of twelve district or eight circuit courts. If someone is found guilty, the case can be appealed before the court of special appeals. If he or she is found guilty again, the person can take the case to the court of appeals. This is the highest court in the state, with seven judges.

and a judicial branch. The Maryland state constitution functions much like the U.S. Constitution. It describes the structure and rules of the state government. The state constitution that Maryland uses today has been in place since 1867.

Annapolis—A Capital City

Annapolis has been Maryland's capital since 1694. "In a few years it will probably be one of the best built cities in America," one English visitor wrote in 1769. Annapolis is one of the oldest state capitals. The governor lives there, and the general assembly meets in the State House for a period of ninety days, beginning each January. Annapolis's State House is the oldest continuously used state house in the nation.

Annapolis was the nation's capital for a short time—from November 1783 to August 1784. After that, the capital was moved to Trenton, New Jersey, and later to New York City and then Philadelphia. In 1789, Maryland and Virginia gave land for a permanent capital city, Washington, D.C.

Construction of the Maryland State House began in 1772. After delays during the American Revolution, the building was finished in 1779.

In Washington, D.C.

Like all citizens, the people of Maryland are represented in the U.S. Congress in Washington, D.C. Each state elects two U.S. senators, who serve six-year terms. There is no limit on the number of terms a U.S. senator can serve.

A state's population determines the number of people that it sends to the U.S. House of Representatives. In 2010, Maryland had eight representatives in the House. They each serve two-year terms and can be elected as many times as voters choose.

How a Bill Becomes a Law

Have you ever wondered how laws are made? They often start out as the ideas of the state's residents. When people think of new laws, they can contact their representatives in the General Assembly. The representatives then write up a proposal called a bill. A bill can start in either the senate or the house of

Congressman Chris Van Hollen (right) speaks to concerned Marylanders during a meeting to discuss health care in 2009.

delegates. If a bill is introduced in the house of delegates, it is read before the whole house. The bill is then presented to the president of the house of delegates, who assigns the bill to a committee. It is the committee's responsibility to hold a hearing to discuss the bill. The committee may amend, or change, the bill. The committee may reject the bill and decide not to present it to the entire house. If the committee members approve the bill, it is sent back to the house. All members of the house of delegates vote on the bill.

Contacting Lawmakers

★ ★ ★ ★ ★ ★ ★ ★ ★ ★ ★ ★ ★

Marylanders who want to express their opinions about an issue that affects their community can visit the official state website at

http://www.maryland.gov

Click on the "State Legislature" link. From there, go to the "Contact or Find a Legislator" pages. Follow the steps to find the name and contact information for any state legislator.

If more than half the house members approve the bill, it goes to the state senate. There, it is discussed, debated, and voted on again. If the senate approves the bill, it is then presented to the governor. He or she may sign the bill or veto—reject—it. If the governor signs it, the bill officially becomes a state law. Even if the governor vetoes the bill, it still has a chance to become a law. The rejected bill goes back to the house and senate for a new vote. If two-thirds of both the house and senate vote to overturn the veto, the bill becomes a law.

Getting Involved

Lawmakers are not the only people who have a say in Maryland's government. Ordinary citizens can do more than suggest ideas to their representatives and vote in elections. They can form citizens' groups and other organizations that promote change. Many people in Maryland are worried about the future. They see the state getting more and more crowded. New homes and business developments are taking up remaining open space. That space could be used for parks and other recreational areas.

An educator from the Chesapeake Bay Foundation leads Maryland students on a canoe trip.

In 1994, people who were concerned about Maryland's future got together. They did not want their state to lose all its open land to homes and businesses, so they formed a group called 1000 Friends of Maryland. The group included businesspeople and environmental groups. Like many activist groups, 1000 Friends of Maryland wants to make the state a better place. They want the government to fix up existing neighborhoods instead of tearing them down. They want to see the government carefully plan new communities without destroying the small amount of open space left in the state.

Another group, the Chesapeake Bay Foundation, fights to make the bay as clean and healthy as it was centuries ago. The group monitors the bay and shares what it learns with businesses, the public, and the government. The group also fights for tougher laws to protect and restore the bay.

Making a Living

Making a living in Maryland can be hard work. But most Marylanders are not complaining. In 2008, Maryland residents earned the fifth-highest average income in the nation.

What do they do? Research and development is a key industry. Maryland is full of doctors, mathematicians, biologists, and other scientists. In fact, Maryland ranks second in the country in the percentage of scientists, technicians, and other professional workers. Eight percent of Maryland workers have jobs in technology. Some work at the many federal agencies headquartered in the state. They may be employed at the Agricultural Research Service in Beltsville, where they work to improve farms. Others are involved in monitoring the weather at the National Weather Service in Silver Spring. Still others work under contract for the government in one of the several research parks that dot the state. The research parks are like college campuses where many companies and institutions can share information on new technologies.

Other Marylanders work in shipping. Foreign goods come and go in the big Port of Baltimore. The port specializes in a kind of cargo transportation called roll-on/roll-off. It is the leading importer of trucks, including farm and construction equipment, which can be driven, or "rolled," off the ship and onto the dock. Baltimore is a good location, because it is within a day's drive of the entire Midwest and its many farms. The port is also the nation's leading

A young Marylander holds a blue crab. The little sea creatures are a big part of the state's economy.

A container cargo ship is unloaded at the Port of Baltimore in 2007.

importer of timber, sugar, and iron ore.

Other Marylanders work in service industries, such as hotels, restaurants, hospitals, resorts, museums, and schools. Some of them serve tourists who spend billions of dollars a year in the state. In 2007, about 27 million tourists spent $13.6 billion in the state.

Agriculture

Farming is big business in Maryland. Farms cover about a third of the state. Tobacco was once the most important crop in Maryland. In 1698, minister Hugh Jones of Calvert County wrote, "Tobacco is our meat, drink, clothing and monies." This is no longer true. As more

Workers & Industries

Industry	Number of People Working in That Industry	Percentage of All Workers Who Are Working in That Industry
Education and health care	619,747	21.8%
Professionals, scientists, and managers	400,068	14.0%
Wholesale and retail businesses	358,904	12.6%
Government	308,576	10.8%
Publishing, media, entertainment, hotels, and restaurants	293,004	10.3%
Construction	226,435	7.9%
Banking and finance, insurance, and real estate	202,086	7.1%
Manufacturing	149,285	5.2%
Other services	143,995	5.1%
Transportation and public utilities	130,010	4.6%
Farming, fishing, forestry, and mining	16,272	0.6%
Totals	**2,848,382**	**100%**

Notes: Figures above do not include people in the armed forces. "Professionals" includes people such as doctors and lawyers. Percentages may not add to 100 because of rounding.

Source: U.S. Bureau of the Census, 2007 estimates

Chickens feed at a farm near Salisbury, Maryland.

Americans understand the harmful effects of smoking cigarettes, tobacco sales are falling. There are fewer than a hundred tobacco farms left, most of which are in the southern part of the state.

Flowers and shrubs grown in nurseries are leading crops in Maryland today. Corn, soybeans, and wheat are also important. Orchards in northern Maryland produce apples, peaches, and other fruits.

Chickens are the state's main livestock product. Some 2.5 million chickens are kept for egg laying. Nearly 300 million, however, are raised for eating. These chickens are called broilers. Have you ever seen chicken that is labeled "Perdue"? Many of these chickens come from the Eastern Shore of Maryland. Perdue Farms started out as a family business and is now the third-largest chicken processor in the United States.

Shell Fishing

Maryland shell fishers, known as watermen, harvest more than 35 million pounds (16 million kilograms) of shellfish in a year. The Chesapeake Bay is famous for its blue crabs. Crab lovers claim the meat is tastier than lobster. Marylanders think so much of their favorite shellfish that in 1989 they named it the state crustacean (shellfish). The shellfish are even featured in a favorite state slogan: "Maryland is for crabs."

Professional crabbers go out into the Chesapeake Bay in their skipjacks. They catch the blue crabs in crab pots. The crab enters a trap in the pot and cannot get out.

People who catch crabs for fun may prefer the old-fashioned long-handled dip net. They wade into the water, and when they see a crab, they dip the net to catch it.

Quick Facts

JIMMY AND SOOK
Decades of tradition have given watermen some colorful lingo. For instance, male crabs are called Jimmy and females are Sook. Pregnant crabs are called Lemon Bellies because of the spongy egg sack they carry. "Dead Man's Fingers" is slang for crab gills.

RECIPE FOR CRAB DIP

Maryland is famous for its crabs. Most people steam the shellfish, crack them open, and enjoy the soft meat inside. The crabmeat can be used in a variety of tasty recipes. Follow this recipe to make a quick and easy crab dip. Ask an adult to help you chop some of the ingredients.

WHAT YOU NEED

2 8-ounce (230 grams) cans Maryland crabmeat, drained and chopped into small pieces

1 8-ounce (230 g) package cream cheese, softened

$1/4$ cup plus 1 tablespoon (60 g) mayonnaise

1 small onion, peeled and minced

$1/4$ teaspoon (1 ml) garlic powder

Place the crabmeat, cream cheese, mayonnaise, onion, and garlic powder in a large bowl and stir until combined.

Transfer the dip to a serving bowl and chill in the refrigerator for at least two hours. Serve with potato chips, crackers, or toast.

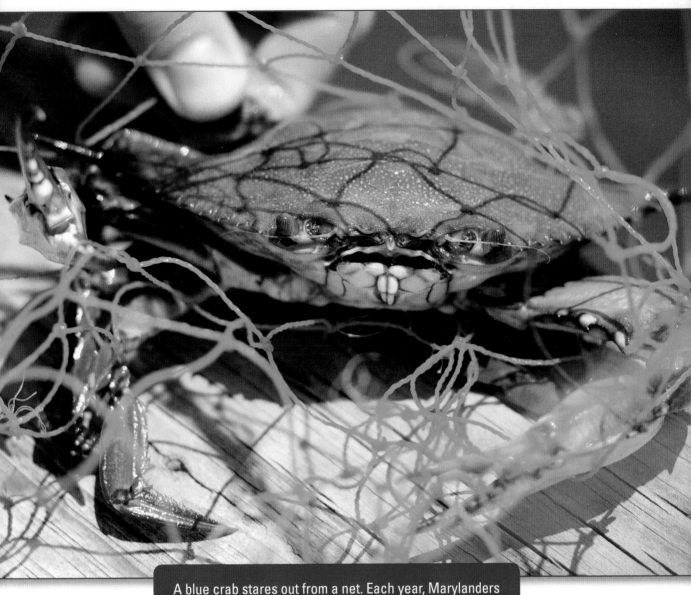

A blue crab stares out from a net. Each year, Marylanders catch millions of pounds of the state crustacean.

Many crabbers also use a hand line, or bait line. This is a long string or fishing line with a weight and bait—often a chicken neck—tied to one end. They lower the line into the water until it reaches the bottom. When a crab begins to nibble on the bait, the crabber carefully pulls up the line and scoops up the crab with a net.

Products & Resources

Chickens

These birds are one of Maryland's most important agricultural products. The state produces nearly 300 million chicken broilers every year.

Power Tools

The Black & Decker Tool Company, headquartered in Towson, has been making tools of all kinds since 1915.

Electronics

From airplane equipment and high-tech weapons to everyday cellular phones, Maryland makes the electronics that change the world.

Fishing

Maryland's fishing industry produces more than $50 million in sales each year. Striped bass, white perch, and menhaden are three of the many kinds of fish caught in the Chesapeake Bay. Shark, bluefish, and flounder are harvested off the Atlantic coast.

Tourism

Tourism is a big business in Maryland. Each year, close to 8 million visitors enjoy the busy boardwalk and white sandy beaches of Ocean City.

Chemical Products

Fertilizer is one of the leading chemical products made in Maryland. Other important chemical products are construction materials, soap, and paint.

Made in Maryland

Manufacturing was once a core part of Maryland's economy. Today, only about one of twenty workers in Maryland has a job in manufacturing. A large number of the state's manufacturers make computers and other high-tech electronics. Interstate 270 in Montgomery County is called the state's high-technology corridor. Other manufacturers package foods, create printing products, or develop chemicals.

Your kitchen spice rack may be filled with spices made by McCormick and Company. This spice company in Sparks, Maryland, was started in 1889 by twenty-five-year-old Willoughby McCormick in a room and cellar in Baltimore.

Defense Industry

Maryland has long played an important role in national defense. The Glenn L. Martin Company in Baltimore produced the famous B-26 bomber and other aircraft that helped the United States win World War II. After a series of mergers, the company is now part of Lockheed Martin, based in Bethesda, Maryland. Hundreds of other aerospace and defense companies have offices in Maryland.

The state's military bases are also major employers. The workforce of military and civilian personnel at Fort Meade alone is close to 40,000 people. The air fleet that transports the U.S. president and other important government leaders is based at Andrews Air Force Base, Maryland, not far from Washington, D.C.

The F-22A Raptor is one of the many high-tech military aircraft produced by Lockheed Martin.

Saving the Environment

Many people in Maryland are concerned about pollution. Waste from factories and sewage systems runs into rivers and the Chesapeake Bay, killing thousands of fish. Overfishing and illegal catching of fish that are too young also hurt the fishing industry. Maryland and neighboring Virginia, Pennsylvania, and Washington, D.C., have formed the Chesapeake Bay Program. The goal of this program is to clean up local waters. Open space is gradually disappearing in Maryland. The state and federal governments are working to save the land left around Baltimore and nearby Washington, D.C. They want to preserve this land for parks and other recreational areas.

Volunteers from government agencies and environmental groups work together to restore the habitat of Barren Island in the Chesapeake Bay.

State Flag & Seal

The Maryland state flag is divided into four sections. The two black-and-gold sections represent the coat of arms of the Calvert family. The Calverts led the first English families who settled in Maryland. The red-and-white sections of the flag represent the Crossland coat of arms. Crossland was the family name of the mother of the first Lord Baltimore, George Calvert. The flag was officially adopted in 1904.

The front side of the state seal shows an armored Lord Baltimore on a horse. However, it is the back side of the seal that is used for official purposes. The back of the seal shows a farmer and a fisherman holding a shield with the Calvert and Crossland coats of arms.

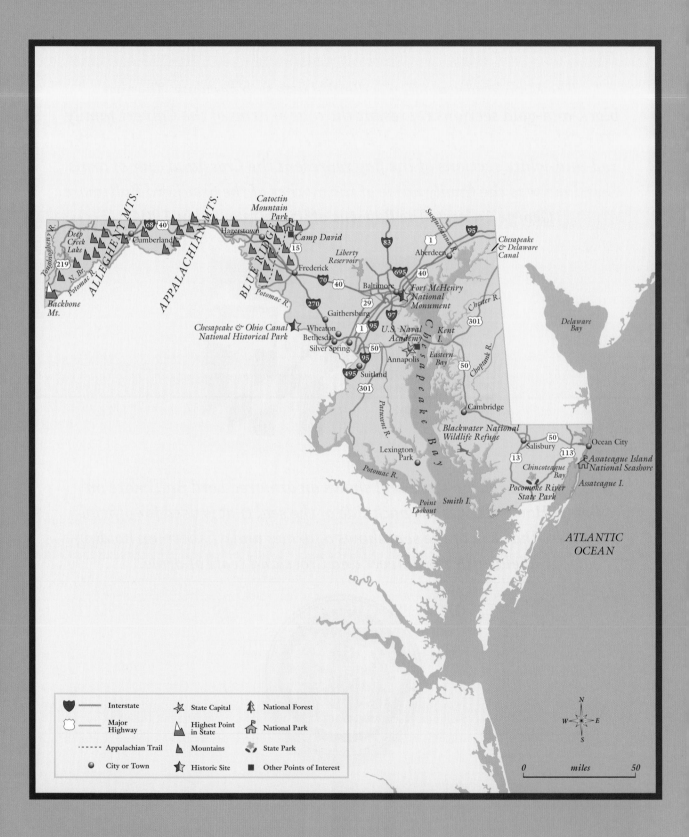

Deep
Creek
Lake

Toughiogheny R.

ALLEGHENY MTS.

68   40

Cumberland

219

N. Br.
Potomac R.

Backbone
Mt.

APPALACHIAN MTS.

Hagerstown

Catoctin
Mountain
Park

Camp David

BLUE RIDGE

15

Frederick

Liberty
Reservoir

Potomac R.

70   40

270

Baltimore

29

83

1

Aberdeen

695

40

Susquehanna R.

95

Chesapeake
& Delaware
Canal

Fort McHenry
National
Monument

Chester R.

301

Delaware
Bay

Gaithersburg

Chesapeake & Ohio Canal
National Historical Park

Wheaton
Bethesda
Silver Spring

1   95

U.S. Naval
Academy

50

95

Annapolis

301

Suitland

495

Patuxent R.

Kent
I.

Eastern
Bay

Chesapeake Bay

50

Choptank R.

Cambridge

Blackwater National
Wildlife Refuge

50

Salisbury

13

Chincoteague
Bay

Pocomoke River
State Park

Assateague I.

Ocean City

113

Assateague Island
National Seashore

Lexington
Park

Potomac R.

Point
Lookout

Smith I.

ATLANTIC
OCEAN

Legend

Interstate	State Capital	National Forest
Major Highway	Highest Point in State	National Park
Appalachian Trail	Mountains	State Park
City or Town	Historic Site	Other Points of Interest

N
W   E
S

0   miles   50

State Song

Maryland, My Maryland

words by James R. Randall
music: "Oh, Tannenbaum"

The des-pot's heel is on thy shore, Mar-y-land, my Mar-y-land! His

torch is at thy tem-ple door, Mar-y-land, my Mar-y-land! A-

venge his pa-tri-o-tic gore That flecked the streets of Balt-i-more, And

be the bat-tle queen of yore, Mar-y-land, my Mar-y-land!

BOOKS

Doak, Robin S. *Maryland, 1634–1776*. Washington, D.C.: National Geographic, 2007.

Kennedy, Mike. *Michael Phelps*. Pleasantville, NY: Gareth Stevens, 2009.

Robinson, J Dennis. *Lord Baltimore: Founder of Maryland*. Minneapolis: Compass Point Books, 2006.

Ruffin, Frances E. *Frederick Douglass: A Powerful Voice for Freedom*. New York: Sterling Publishing, 2008.

Tayac, Gabrielle, and John Harrington. *Meet Naiche: a Native Boy from the Chesapeake Bay Area*. Tulsa, OK: Council Oak Books, 2006.

WEBSITES

Maryland Department of Natural Resources for Kids:
http://www.dnr.state.md.us/mydnr

Maryland Judiciary Kids' Page:
http://www.courts.state.md.us/kidspage/index.html

Maryland Kids' Page:
http://www.mdkidspage.org

Maryland State Archives — Guide to Government Records:
http://guide.mdsa.net/viewer.cfm?page=mdgov

Steven Otfinoski has written more than ninety fiction and nonfiction books for young readers. His previous works for Marshall Cavendish include books on states, history, and animals. Otfinoski lives in Connecticut with his wife, a high school teacher and an editor.

Andy Steinitz has written and edited educational and reference materials for *The World Almanac*, Borders Books, and *The New York Times*. As a child, he took trips with his family to the Eastern Shore and Baltimore's Inner Harbor. Maryland's blue crabs are one of his favorite foods. He currently works at Pratt Institute. He lives in Brooklyn, NY.

Page numbers in **boldface** are illustrations.